Published by

CCC Publications
21630 Lassen Street
Chatsworth, CA 91311

Copyright © 1994 Don Smith

Manufactured in the United States of America

Cover © 1994 CCC Publications

Interior illustrations © 1994 CCC Publications

Cover & Interior art by Don Smith

ISBN: 0-918259-73-8

If your local U.S. bookstore is out of stock, copies of this book may be obtained by mailing check or money order for $4.99 per book (plus $2.50 to cover postage and handling) to: CCC Publications; 21630 Lassen St.; Chatsworth, CA 91311.

Pre-publication Edition – 5/94

THE OFFICE FROM HELL

INTRODUCTION

THE OFFICE FROM HELL PROBABLY NEEDS NO INTRODUCTION BECAUSE ANYONE WHO HAS EVER WORKED IN AN OFFICE ANY TIME, ANYWHERE, WILL RECOGNIZE CO-WORKERS AND BOSSES WHO SEEM TO HAVE COME FROM SOME EPISODE OF "THE TWILIGHT ZONE." A FEW UNLUCKY SOULS LIVE IN THE OFFICE FROM HELL DAY IN AND DAY OUT… BUT EVEN THE BEST OFFICE HAS ITS HELLISH DAYS. SO DESCEND WITH US NOW TO THE SIXTH RING OF "THE INFERNO," ESPECIALLY DESIGNATED FOR THOSE NERDS, GOOF-OFFS, DWEEBS AND FIENDS WHO SOMETIMES MAKE YOUR LIFE A NIGHTMARE. YOU'LL SEE MANY FAMILIAR FACES AND IF YOU LOOK CLOSELY, WHO KNOWS, YOU MIGHT EVEN FIND YOURSELF.

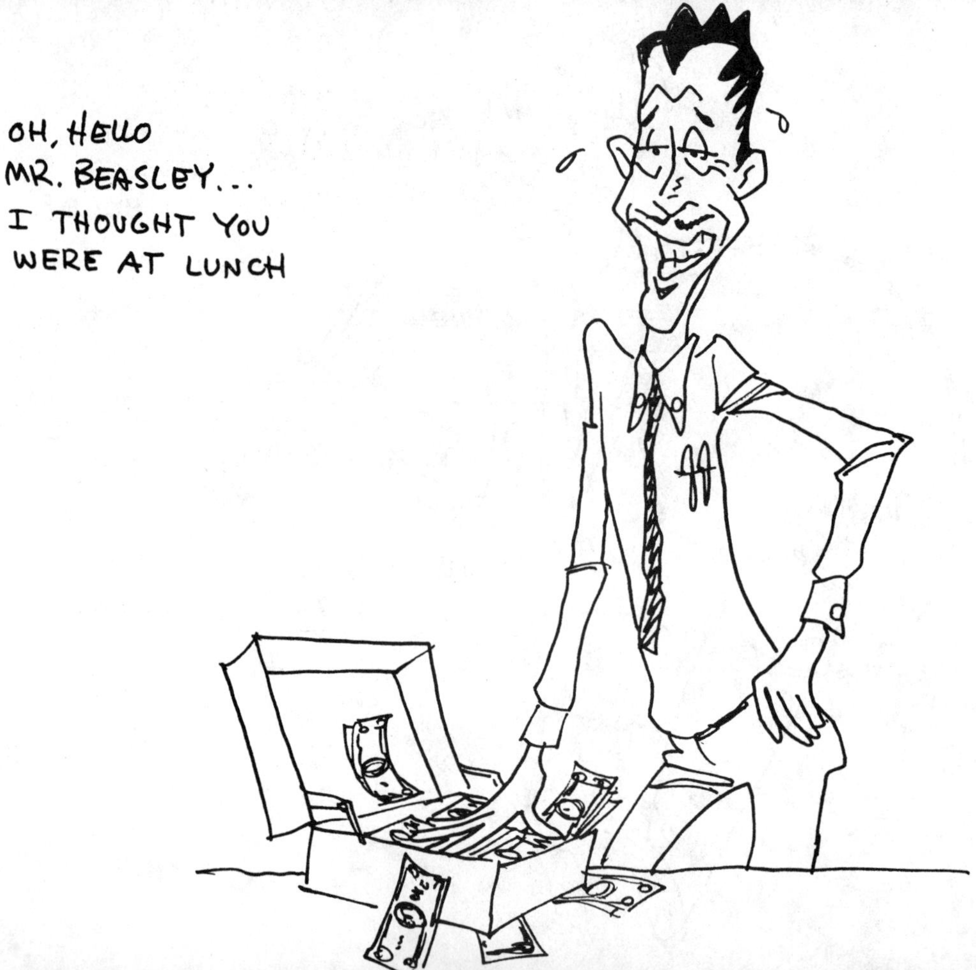
OH, HELLO MR. BEASLEY... I THOUGHT YOU WERE AT LUNCH

CAN SOMEBODY
CATCH THE PHONE
FOR AN HOUR?

I GOTTA TYPE
A LETTER

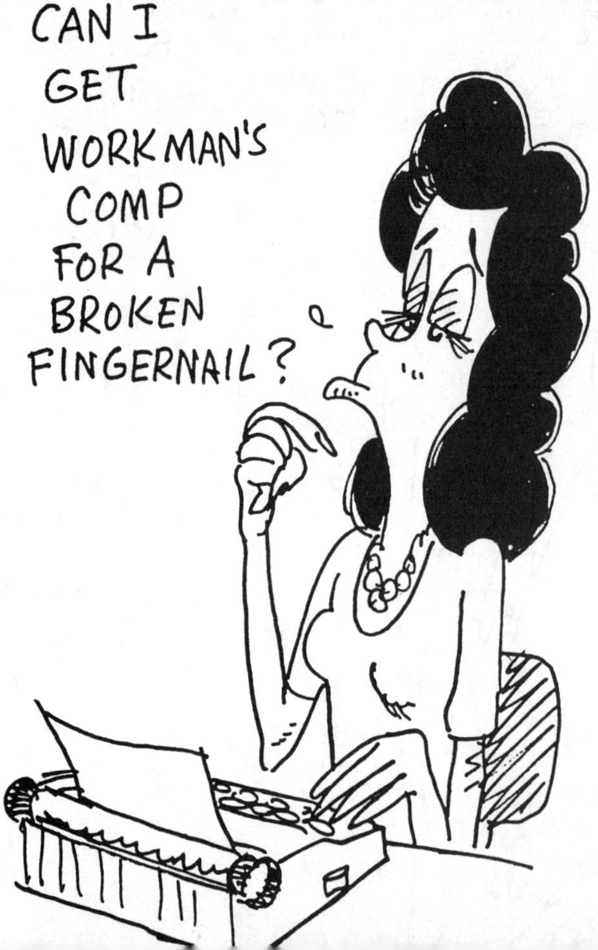
CAN I GET WORKMAN'S COMP FOR A BROKEN FINGERNAIL?

I HOPE THIS ISN'T ONE OF THOSE OFFICES WHERE THERE'S A LOT OF PRESSURE TO BE GOOD.

I SHOULDA
BEEN HERE
AT EIGHT?
WHY? DID
I MISS
SOMETHING?

THOSE LITTLE
COLORED TABS
WERE
CLASHING!
SO I
MOVED ALL
THE FILES
AROUND
AND NOW
THEY'RE
COLOR
COORDINATED
AND THEY'RE
LOVELY!

YOU WANT SOMEONE
WHO CAN TYPE !! OH !
I THOUGHT YOU JUST
WANTED SOMEONE
WHO WAS FAST!

LOOK, SMEDLY, YOU'RE THE FIRST ONE HERE EVERY MORNING. THE LAST ONE TO LEAVE IN THE EVENING. YOU NEVER TAKE LUNCH. NEVER ASK FOR A VACATION... JUST WHAT ARE YOU UP TO!!?

DON'T WORRY
ABOUT ME..
I MARCH TO
A DIFFERENT
DRUMMER

DON'T JUST
SIT THERE, MISS SMALLY,
XEROX SOMETHING!

HOW'S MY BIG OLE HANDSOME MAN?
HELLO - HOLD PLEASE
I MISS YOUR HUGGY WUGGUMS
HELLO - HOLD PLEASE
DOES OO MISS YOUR SWEETUMS?

AFTER YOU'VE BEEN
HERE AWHILE YOU
REALIZE THAT BENEATH
THAT GRUFF EXTERIOR
LIES A HEART OF SOLID
GRANITE.

THIS IS
BILL'S MOTHER.
I KNOW HE'S
SUPPOSED TO
BE THERE AT 8,
BUT HE GOT IN
LATE LAST NIGHT
AND I JUST
HATE TO WAKE
HIM.

I REALLY NEEDED
THIS JOB...
I HAVEN'T BEEN ABLE
TO GET ANYTHING
SINCE I SUED
MY LAST BOSS.

HEY,
WHERE'S
THE BROOM?
I NEED TO
FINISH
PUTTIN' THE
TRUCK IN
THE GARAGE

DEAR MOM,
I WISH MIZ
RATZBURGER,
MY 12TH GRADE
ENGLISH TICHER
CUD SEE ME NOW.
SHE SED I'D
NEVER GET
ENNYWHERE!
BUT HEER
I ARE, A
SEKRYTERRY.

THE
LAST PLACE
I WORKED,
I WAS
THE
LOOKOUT

OF COURSE I'M
RESPONSIBLE!
ON MY LAST JOB
THEY BLAMED ME
FOR EVERYTHING!

OK! SO
WHICH WAY
   IS THE
SECRETARIAL POOL?

THEY
MADE ME
ROUTING
SUPERVISOR
`CAUSE I LIKE
TELLIN' PEOPLE
WHERE TO GO.

FIRST
THINGS
FIRST.
WHERE'S
THE
MICROWAVE?

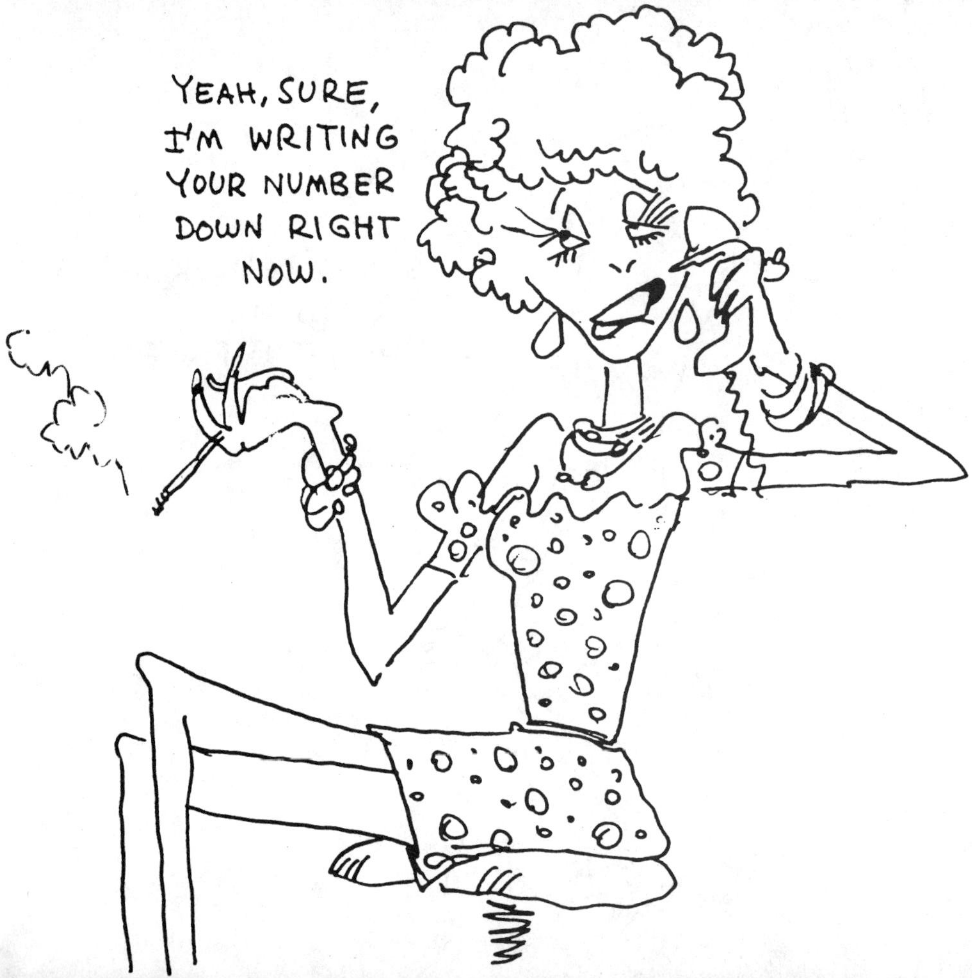
YEAH, SURE,
I'M WRITING
YOUR NUMBER
DOWN RIGHT
NOW.

YOU NEED
SOMEBODY
FOR A HIGH
LEVEL
POSITION?

OH GOLLY!
I BROKE A
FINGERNAIL
ON THIS BAD
OLE TYPEWRITER.
HAVEN'T YA GOT
SOMETHIN' ELSE
I COULD DO?

ABOUT THE "AUTHOR"

Don Smith owns an ad agency and design studio where he met many of the characters in this book. His humorous illustrations have been used on billboards, record jackets, packages, advertising and in books — including many published by CCC. Don also has a long-running cartoon called, "It's a Weird World," that appears in his local paper.

"We all believe everyone in the world, (except us) is weird..." says Smith, "so it really doesn't take much exaggeration on my part to caricature the people I observe."

Maybe you can sleep better at night knowing that Don is keeping an eye out for the weirdos. Or maybe not.

TITLES BY CCC PUBLICATIONS

NEW PARTY BOOKS (Available: May 1994)

Retail $4.95
THINGS YOU CAN DO WITH A USELESS MAN
FLYING FUNNIES
MARITAL BLISS & OTHER OXYMORONS
THE VERY VERY SEXY DOT-TO-DOT BOOK
BASTARD'S GUIDE TO BUSINESS SURVIVAL
THE DEFINITIVE FART BOOK
THE TOTAL WIMP'S GUIDE TO SEX
THE CAT OWNER'S SHAPE-UP MANUAL
LIFE'S MOST EMBARRASSING MOMENTS
PMS CRAZED: TOUCH ME & I'LL KILL YOU!
RETIRED: LET THE GAMES BEGIN
MALE BASHING: WOMEN'S FAVORITE PASTIME
THE OFFICE FROM HELL
FOOD & SEX
BUT OSSIFER, IT'S NOT MY FAULT
YOU KNOW YOU'RE AN OLD FART WHEN...
HOW TO REALLY PARTY!!!
HOW TO SURVIVE A JEWISH MOTHER – **Oct.**

1994 NEW TRADE PAPERBACKS – Retail $4.95
SHARING THE ROAD WITH IDIOTS
GREATEST ANSWERING MACHINE MESSAGES

1001 WAYS TO PROCRASTINATE – **May**
FITNESS FANATICS – **Jun.**
THE WORLD'S GREATEST PUT-DOWN LINES – **Jun.**
HORMONES FROM HELL II – **May**
YOUNGER MEN ARE BETTER THAN RETIN-A – **Jul.**
RED HOT MONOGAMY – **($6.95) Jul.**
ROSS PEROT: DON'T QUOTE ME – **Sep.**

BEST SELLING TRADE PAPERBACKS – Retail $4.95
HORMONES FROM HELL **($5.95)**
KILLER BRAS & OTHER HAZARDS OF THE 50'S
BETTER TO BE OVER THE HILL THAN UNDER IT
HUSBANDS FROM HELL
HOW TO ENTERTAIN PEOPLE YOU HATE
THE UGLY TRUTH ABOUT MEN
WHAT DO WE DO NOW??
TALK YOUR WAY OUT OF A TRAFFIC TICKET
THE BOTTOM HALF

BEST SELLING TRADE PAPERBACKS – Retail $3.95
NO HANG-UPS
NO HANG-UPS II
NO HANG-UPS III
GETTING EVEN WITH THE ANSWERING MACHINE

NEVER A DULL CARD
WORK SUCKS!
THE PEOPLE WATCHER'S FIELD GUIDE
THE UNOFFICIAL WOMEN'S DIVORCE GUIDE
YOUR GUIDE TO CORPORATE SURVIVAL
THE ABSOLUTE LAST CHANCE DIET BOOK
FOR MEN ONLY (How To Survive Marriage)
SUPERIOR PERSON'S GUIDE TO IRRITATIONS
GIFTING RIGHT
HOW TO GET EVEN WITH YOUR EXes
HOW TO SUCCEED IN SINGLES BARS
OUTRAGEOUS BUMPER-SNICKERS **($2.95)**

ACCESSORIES
THE GUILT BAG **($4.95)**
THE "MAGIC BOOKMARK" BOOK COVER **($2.95)**

NO HANG-UPS – CASSETTES – Retail $4.98
Vol. I: GENERAL MESSAGES
Vol. II: BUSINESS MESSAGES
Vol. III: 'R' RATED MESSAGES
Vol. IV: SOUND EFFECTS ONLY
Vol. V: CELEBRI-TEASE